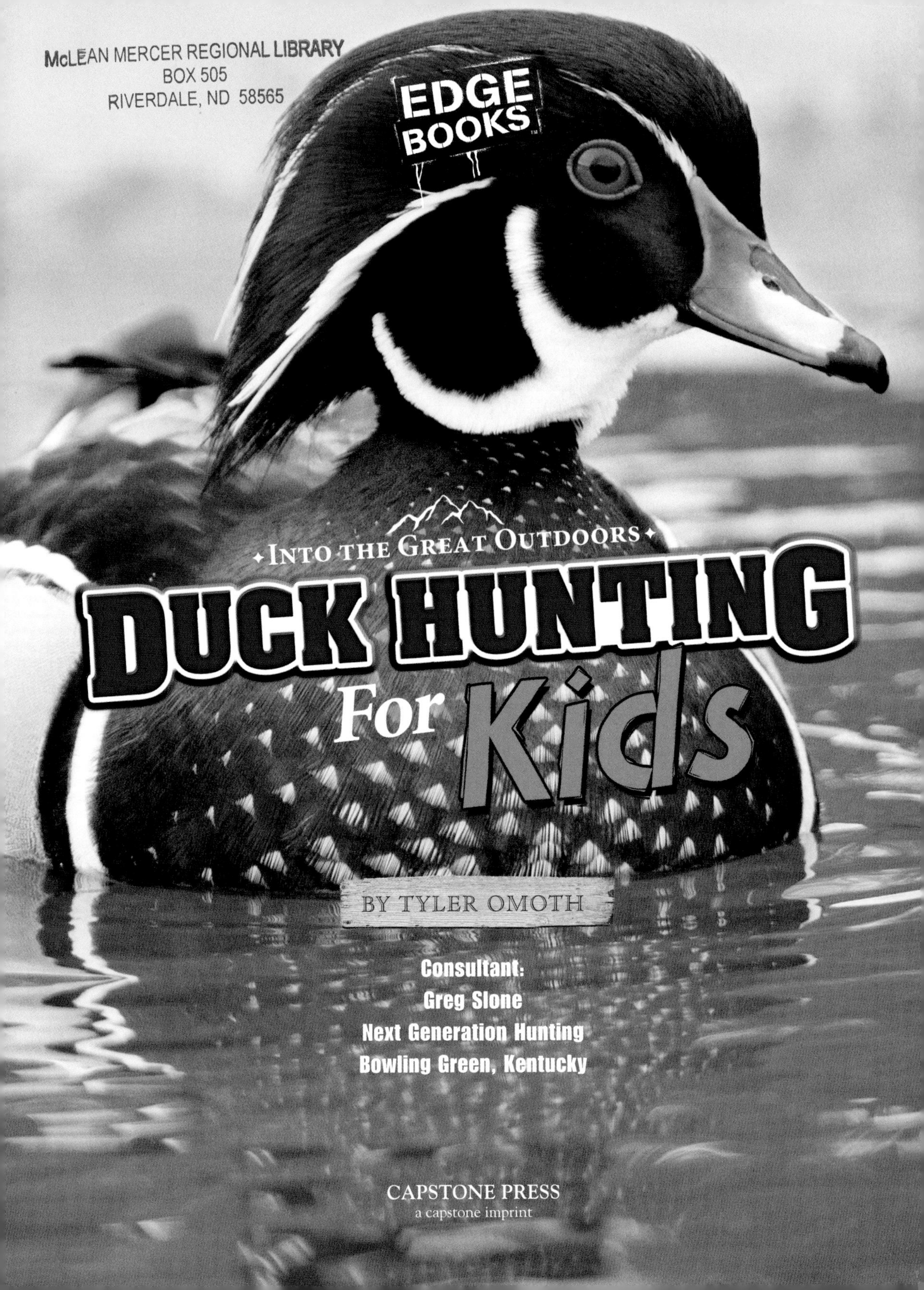

EDGE
BOOKS

✦ INTO THE GREAT OUTDOORS ✦

DUCK HUNTING
For Kids

BY TYLER OMOTH

Consultant:
Greg Slone
Next Generation Hunting
Bowling Green, Kentucky

CAPSTONE PRESS
a capstone imprint

Edge Books are published by Capstone Press,
1710 Roe Crest Drive, North Mankato, Minnesota 56003.
www.capstonepub.com

Library of Congress Cataloging-in-Publication Data
Omoth, Tyler.
  Duck hunting for kids / by Tyler Omoth.
    p. cm.—(Edge Books. Into the great outdoors)
  Includes bibliographical references and index.
  Summary: "Explores the sport of duck hunting, including its rich history,
specific gear, special techniques, safety requirements, and conservation
efforts"—Provided by publisher.
  ISBN 978-1-4296-8616-7 (library binding)
  ISBN 978-1-4296-9268-7 (paperback)
  ISBN 978-1-62065-226-8 (ebook PDF)
  1. Duck shooting—Juvenile literature. I. Title.
  SK333.D8O46 2013
  799.2'44—dc23   2011051837

Editorial Credits
Christopher L. Harbo, editor; Ted Williams, designer; Marcie Spence,
    media researcher; Sarah Schuette, photo stylist; Marcy Morin,
    scheduler; Laura Manthe, production specialist

Photo Credits
Art Resource, N.Y.: Smithsonian American Art Museum, Washington, DC,
6; Capstone Studio: Karon Dubke, 4–5, 6–7, 10, 13, 14, 19, 20–21, 22, 24;
Corbis: Mike Kemp, 28; iStockphoto: PaulTessier, 9, WilliamSherman, 18;
Shutterstock: Andrejs Jegorovs, 8–9, donatas1205, design element, Geanina
Bechea, 3, Iakov Kalinin, 26, Julie Lubick, 1, Kirk Geisler, 15, Maslov Dmitry,
28–29, MaxyM, design element, Mircea Bezergheanu, 16, papkin, cover,
SoleilC, design element, Steve Byland, 8, Zadiraka Evgenii, design element;
War Eagle Boats by Team Ward, Inc.: 25

Printed in the United States of America in Stevens Point, Wisconsin.
032012   006678WZF12

TABLE OF CONTENTS

CHAPTER 1

BAGGING A DUCK

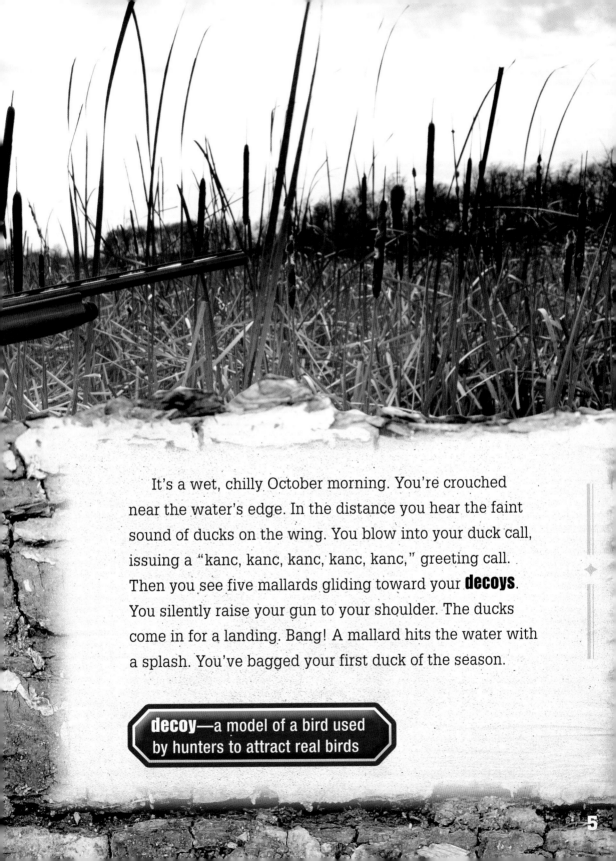

It's a wet, chilly October morning. You're crouched near the water's edge. In the distance you hear the faint sound of ducks on the wing. You blow into your duck call, issuing a "kanc, kanc, kanc, kanc, kanc," greeting call. Then you see five mallards gliding toward your **decoys**. You silently raise your gun to your shoulder. The ducks come in for a landing. Bang! A mallard hits the water with a splash. You've bagged your first duck of the season.

decoy—a model of a bird used by hunters to attract real birds

HISTORY

Before European settlers came to North America, American Indians hunted ducks for food. At that time, there were hundreds of millions of ducks. When European settlers arrived, they began hunting ducks to sell for profit. Without laws, hunters took all the birds they could shoot. By the late 1800s, market hunting had caused duck numbers to drop dramatically in North America.

In the early 1900s, market hunting became illegal and duck populations began to rise. But disaster struck when a drought began drying up U.S. **wetlands**. By 1930 the drought had almost destroyed duck populations nationwide. To increase the populations, the U.S. government passed the Migratory Bird Hunting Stamp Act of 1934. This law required duck hunters to buy a duck stamp. Money raised from the stamps was used to buy and protect wetlands. These protected wetlands helped increase duck populations.

wetland—an area of land covered by water and plants; marshes, swamps, and bogs are wetlands

FACT
A duck disaster occurred on December 25, 1947. Because of strong currents and heavy fog, nearly 1,000 unsuspecting ducks were swept over Niagara Falls.

Today very few people hunt ducks for profit. The sport of duck hunting is alive and well. Thanks to hunting regulations and **conservation** efforts, more than 45 million ducks live in North America. Hunters are able to enjoy one of their favorite pastimes each season.

conservation—the protection of animals and plants, as well as the wise use of what we get from nature

mallards

harlequins

wood duck

Duck Species

North America has at least 36 **species** of ducks. These species are divided into dabbling and diving ducks. Dabbling ducks are also called puddle ducks. They like shallow waters such as ponds, rivers, and small lakes. Shallow water allows them to reach their food by dipping their heads underwater. Mallards and wood ducks are common dabbling ducks. Diving ducks catch their food by diving underwater. They usually like large lakes and even oceans. Redheads, canvasbacks, and harlequins are diving ducks.

species—a group of plants or animals that share common characteristics

FACT
The long-tailed duck is one of the best divers of all. It can dive more than 200 feet (61 meters) deep!

CHAPTER 2

DUCK HUNTING GEAR

Being prepared is key for a successful hunt. That means having the right hunting gear. Choosing the right gun, clothing, and duck call will help you bag your **limit** of ducks.

Shotguns and Shells

A gun is a hunter's most important tool. Choose one that is comfortable for you. Shotguns are used for duck hunting because they use birdshot. Birdshot shells are packed with small beads that spread out as they fly through the air. The spreading shot makes it easier to hit moving targets and does less damage to the bird. Most duck hunters use either 12-gauge or 20-gauge shotguns. Young hunters may want to start with a 20-gauge shotgun. The 20-gauge is a smaller gun, so it is easier to carry and fire. It also has less recoil, which means it won't kick back as hard when you fire it.

limit—the number of ducks a hunter can legally kill and take home in one day

Choosing the right shotgun shells is also important to bagging a duck. Federal law requires hunters to use steel birdshot when hunting ducks and other wetland birds. Small size 6 shot is a good choice for small ducks at close range. Larger size 2 and 3 shot works better for larger ducks and longer range shots.

Hunting Clothes

Ducks have very good eyesight. If they spot you tucked into the reeds along the edge of a lake, they may not land. **Camouflage** clothing is a must for hunting ducks. When choosing jackets, hats, gloves, and facemasks, look for a camouflage pattern that matches your hunting area. If the plant life is still green, you'll want a green-based camo pattern. Brown works better later in the season. Some hunting clothes are reversible so they can work for different surroundings.

Duck hunters also hunt in or around wetlands. They often need to wade through water. It pays to have a good pair of chest waders. Neoprene waders will help keep you warm and dry as you walk through wetlands.

FACT
Ducks can see almost everything above, below, in front, and behind them at one time. They also can focus on near and distant objects at the same time.

camouflage—coloring or covering that makes animals, people, and objects look like their surroundings

Duck Calls

The two main types of duck calls are double reed and single reed. The double reed call is the best choice for beginning hunters. Blowing through the call's two reeds is easy to do and makes the raspy sound hens make. The single reed takes a lot more practice, but it also makes a wider variety of duck sounds.

Duck hunters try to make the right sound for each hunting situation. The basic quack is the first call you should learn. This single note with a crisp ending is an easy way to lure in ducks. Hunters also bring in ducks with a greeting call. This short burst of 5 to 7 notes in an even rhythm gets lower with each note.

If ducks don't come to a greeting call, a comeback call is a good choice. This call is a louder series of 5 to 7 notes that gets faster. Sometimes this call will get birds that have passed you to turn around.

HUNTING DOGS

Duck hunters often rely on labrador and golden retrievers to bring in ducks. Labrador retrievers are large, strong dogs with a natural **instinct** to retrieve. On the hunt, they don't mind diving into icy water to bring in a duck. Golden retrievers are slightly smaller than labs. They love swimming and have a waterproof coat that makes them excellent duck hunting dogs.

labrador
retriever

instinct—behavior that is natural rather than learned

Every successful hunt starts with a good plan. Plan your hunting strategy according to the season and whether you're hunting from land or on the water.

Seasons

Duck hunting seasons usually match up with **migration**. During this time, ducks fly from colder areas to warmer areas to find their winter homes. Each state has its own hunting seasons and regulations. But as a general rule, duck hunting seasons start in the fall and last into early winter. Most states have seasons or weekends during which young hunters can hunt with an adult. These times are great opportunities for younger hunters to bag a few ducks without a lot of competition from other hunters.

> **migration**—the regular movement of animals as they search different places for food

Blinds

Using a duck blind is one of the best ways to stay hidden on a hunt. Land blinds should be close to the water and tucked into reeds or tall grass. Because ducks land while flying into the wind, set up the duck blind with your back to the wind.

Some hunters attach blinds to the top of their boats. Boat blinds blend in with shoreline grasses and keep you hidden right on the water. A boat also allows you to retrieve any ducks you shoot over the water.

Decoys

Decoy hunting is a good technique for drawing
ducks into lakes and ponds with room to land. The
key to decoy hunting is making your spread of decoys
look real. Place a mix of duck types, such as mallards,
ringnecks, and drakes, in an open area of water. Be
sure your decoys face different directions. Doing so
will make them look more natural. Also consider using
decoys with bobbing heads and flapping wings.

Shooting Techniques

Duck hunters use jump shooting or pass shooting techniques. Jump shooting uses the element of surprise. To jump shoot, you sneak up on ducks sitting in a pond or lake. The goal is to get as close as possible before the ducks see you. Once they take flight, you'll be close enough to take a shot.

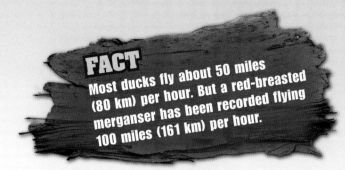

For pass shooting, you wait for the ducks to come to you. Start by setting up your blind in an area where you've seen ducks fly by in the past. As the ducks fly over on their usual flight pattern, you take your shot. But for pass shooting to work, you have to be patient. Shooting at birds out of range is called skybursting. Skybursting leads to wasted shots and injured birds. Practice your shooting skills by target shooting or trap shooting before a hunt. That way you'll know the best distance for taking a shot.

Safety should be considered every time you hunt. Duck hunting is no exception because it is usually done near water and involves guns. A few simple safety rules must always be followed.

General Safety

Duck hunters should follow a few basic safety precautions every time they hunt. Before you set out, pack a basic survival kit. It can include a cell phone, water, rope, first-aid supplies, a knife, and a waterproof fire-starting kit. Also, tell someone where and how long you plan to hunt.

Gun Safety

No matter where or how you hunt, gun safety is always important. During a hunt, be sure to keep the gun barrel pointed away from yourself or other hunters. Be sure to keep the **safety** switch on until you're ready to fire at ducks.

safety—a device that prevents a gun from firing

FACT

In the United States, more than 12 million people hunt wild game each year. More than 2 million of those people hunt ducks and other migratory birds.

Before you shoot, consider what is behind your target. You don't want to fire at other hunters or buildings accidentally. When hunting in groups, be sure everyone is either standing or sitting. Otherwise seated hunters could hit other hunters standing in front of them.

Boat Safety

Hunting on the water requires a few extra safety precautions. As you pack your boat, avoid overloading it with gear or people. An overloaded boat can easily tip over on choppy water. When you are on the water, always wear a life jacket. Be sure to shoot from a seated position as well. This way the gun's recoil won't knock you over the side of the boat.

CHAPTER 5

CONSERVATION

Duck hunting is a traditional sport that many families pass from one generation to the next. For this sport to continue, both hunters and organizations must work to preserve wetlands and duck populations.

Hunting Conservation

Ducks need wetlands for food, nesting, and raising their young. When hunting, always leave the area just as you found it. Don't litter or change the area any more than is necessary. Keeping wetlands as natural as possible will encourage ducks to return every year.

Protecting duck populations also requires you to hunt responsibly. That means never taking more than your legal limit of ducks. Also, don't shoot at ducks that are out of your range. You may wound them and hurt their chances to survive.

Organizations

Some organizations work to protect wetlands and duck populations across North America. Ducks Unlimited is one of the largest conservation groups in the United States. It started raising money to preserve wetlands in 1937. Since then, Ducks Unlimited has improved or preserved more than 70 million acres (28 million hectares) of wetlands in North America.

The Delta Waterfowl Foundation also focuses on wetland and waterfowl conservation. Started in 1911, Delta Waterfowl raises money for the research of waterfowl populations. The organization also places hen houses in wetlands to give ducks safe places to nest.

DUCK STAMPS

The Federal Duck Stamp program is one way that the U.S. government raises money to buy and protect waterfowl wetlands. Each fall the program holds an art contest to design the next year's stamp. Hunters must buy the stamp along with their license. But some people buy the artistic stamp purely as a donation or to keep as a collector's item. In 1989 the Federal Junior Duck Stamp Conservation and Design Program began. In 1993 this program began issuing junior stamps to encourage younger hunters to help with conservation efforts.

GLOSSARY

camouflage (KA-muh-flahzh)—coloring or covering that makes animals, people, and objects look like their surroundings

conservation (kon-sur-VAY-shuhn)—the protection of animals and plants, as well as the wise use of nature

decoy (DEE-koi)—a model of a bird used by hunters to attract real birds

instinct (IN-stingkt)—behavior that is natural rather than learned

limit (LIM-it)—the number of ducks a hunter can legally kill and take home in one day

migration (mye-GRAY-shuhn)—the regular movement of animals as they search different places for food

safety (SAYF-tee)—a device that prevents a gun from firing

species (SPEE-sheez)—a group of animals or plants that share common characteristics

wetland (WET-land)—an area of land covered by water and plants; marshes, swamps, and bogs are wetlands

READ MORE

Frahm, Randy. *Duck Hunting.* The Great Outdoors. Mankato, Minn.: Capstone Press, 2008.

MacRae, Sloan. *Waterfowl Hunting.* Open Season. New York: PowerKids Press, 2011.

Wolny, Philip. *Waterfowl.* Hunting, Pursuing Wild Game! New York: Rosen Central, 2011.

INTERNET SITES

FactHound offers a safe, fun way to find Internet sites related to this book. All of the sites on FactHound have been researched by our staff.

Here's all you do:

Visit *www.facthound.com*

Type in this code: 9781429686167

Check out projects, games and lots more at
www.capstonekids.com

INDEX